TAKING PART

Brad Pitt

Paula Guzzetti

DILLON PRESS
Parsippany, New Jersey

Photo Credits
Front cover: Theo Kinma/Shooting Star.
Back cover: I.P.A./Stills/Retna.

Columbia, Missouri Chamber of Commerce: 20. The Gamma Liaison Network: 64; Allen: 55; Barry King: 5, 28, 30. Photofest: 1, 14, 15, 34, 35, 36, 39, 41, 43, 45, 47, 49, 51, 53. Seth Poppel Yearbook Archives: 12, 17. Retna, Ltd./Bill Davila: 3; I.P.A./Stills: 52; Michael Putland: 6; Stills: 57. Springfield, Missouri Convention & Visitors Bureau: 8. Superstock: 24. University of Missouri Publications & Alumni Communication: 19.

Library of Congress Cataloging-in-Publication Data
Guzzetti, Paula.
  Brad Pitt/by Paula Guzzetti. —1st ed.
   p. cm.— (Taking part books)
  Includes index.
  Summary: Discusses the life and career of the popular film actor who has become a superstar.
  ISBN 0-382-39795-9 (LSB). —ISBN 0-382-39796-7 (scr)
  1. Pitt, Brad, 1963– —Juvenile literature. 2. Actors— United States—Biography—Juvenile literature. [1. Pitt, Brad, 1963– .
 2. Actors and actresses.] I. Title.
PN2287.P54G89   1998
791.43'028'092–dc21
[B]   97-16684

Copyright © 1998 by Paula Guzzetti
Cover and book design: Michelle Farinella

All rights reserved. No part of this book may be reproduced or transmitted in any form or by any means, electronic or mechanical, including photocopying, recording, or by any information storage and retrieval system, without permission in writing from the Publisher.

Published by Dillon Press
A Division of Simon & Schuster
299 Jefferson Road, Parsippany, NJ 07054

First Edition
Printed in the United States of America
10 9 8 7 6 5 4 3 2 1

CONTENTS

CHAPTER 1
A Star Is Born 7

CHAPTER 2
A Missouri Childhood 9

CHAPTER 3
A Daring Decision 18

CHAPTER 4
Making It in Hollywood 23

CHAPTER 5
Television and Movies 29

CHAPTER 6
J.D. and Beyond 38

CHAPTER 7
The Actor and the Man 50

INDEX 62

Brad Pitt in an early publicity shot

CHAPTER 1

A Star Is Born

Brad Pitt arrived in Hollywood in 1986. Fresh from Missouri, he was just 22 years old. His dream was to make it big in films. Anyone assessing his chances would have thought them slim. He had no training in acting. Except for a few school plays, he had no acting experience. He didn't know anyone in the movie business. And competition from hundreds of other young Hollywood hopefuls would be tough.

Yet, within seven months of his arrival, Brad had his first television role. Four years later he was on his way to becoming a movie superstar.

Brad's rapid rise to fame was due, at least in part, to his natural talent and good looks. But it was also the result of his upbringing. Raised to follow his heart, he made his career moves on instinct. For a less secure person, such a daring course could have proved disastrous. For cool and confident Brad, however, it was exactly the right approach.

Lake Springfield, one of the many scenic spots near Brad's Missouri home

CHAPTER 2

A Missouri Childhood

William Bradley Pitt was born on December 18, 1963. He spent his first years in the town of Shawnee, Oklahoma, where his father managed a trucking company. Before Brad turned three, his family moved to Missouri. They settled in Springfield, a lively city sheltered in the foothills of the Ozark Mountains. It was a beautiful region, which Brad would later explore and come to love.

The family was happy in Springfield. Brad's father, Bill, worked hard at his business, and Brad's mother, Jane, worked as a counselor and managed the household. And a busy household it was. In addition to Brad and his parents, the family included Brad's younger brother, Doug, and younger sister, Julie.

In many ways Brad had a traditional American upbringing. Reared in the American heartland, he was taught to value family, religion, good manners, and hard work. He learned his lessons well. By all accounts he was a loving and obedient child who gave his best to

BRAD PITT

everything he tried. The piano accompanist at Brad's church remembers Brad as a six-year-old singing his heart out in the church choir. "You couldn't keep from watching Brad," she recalled in an article in the January 30, 1995, issue of *People* magazine, "because his face was so expressive. He would move his little mouth so big with all the words that he attracted everyone's attention." In the same article the assistant principal of Brad's school described Brad as "a super kid"—the kind of polite, eager, and high-achieving student who is every teacher's dream.

But Brad's traditional upbringing was not meant to inhibit him or to interfere with his fun. His parents simply viewed it as a basic grounding for life. Brad was free to remain on this traditional path or to find his own way. His mother and father were warm and loving people who wanted nothing more than their children's happiness. Above all else, Brad was encouraged to be true to himself and to do what he enjoyed.

Brad's mother believed that he had many talents. "She just thought it from Day 1," Brad told *Rolling Stone* magazine in December of 1994. Her unwavering support built his confidence. It also gave him the courage to keep trying new things. In addition to singing

A Missouri Childhood

in the church choir, he was involved in activities at school. At Springfield's Kickapoo High, he joined the school chorus, participated in debates and student government, and took part in school plays, although only in supporting roles. (His fascination with acting would come later.)

For a while he also tried sports. His dedication to baseball won him a permanent scar on his left cheekbone when he tried to catch a pop fly that had become obscured by the sun. "I still threw the guy out on second after it dropped on my face," he noted in *Rolling Stone*'s December 1, 1994, issue.

He even showed this same determination in tennis, a game that he didn't particularly like. It was during an especially grueling match that his father gave him a crucial piece of advice that would remain with him for years to come. Brad recalled his father's words in the same *Rolling Stone* article.

"Are you having fun?" Bill Pitt asked, as Brad stomped off the court in disgust.

"No," Brad answered.

"Then don't do it," his father replied.

Those four simple words would become a guiding force in Brad's life.

BRAD PITT

*A teenage Brad, hard at work
on the tennis court*

Besides helping Brad find his true course, his parents also introduced him to the joys of adventure and travel. Whenever Bill Pitt could manage time away from work, he took the family camping. The Ozarks were a favorite

A Missouri Childhood

destination. Brad came to love those outings, as much for the freedom of the open road as for the magnificent scenery. Later, when he turned 16 and was given the family's old Buick, he revisited the sites alone. He also traveled beyond the familiar territory to more distant spots. It was the beginning of his desire to venture forth on his own and to see the world beyond his home.

It was also through his parents that Brad came to appreciate films. On hot summer evenings when Brad was small, Bill and Jane Pitt would pile the children into the family car and head for the drive-in movie. Equipped with Kool-Aid and a bucket of popcorn, Brad would settle himself on the car hood and allow the sounds and images of the huge outdoor screen to work their magic. The first film he remembers seeing was a western called *Butch Cassidy and the Sundance Kid,* starring Paul Newman and Robert Redford. Brad was just six years old at the time and liked the film for its stars and its action.

Years later he was enthralled by a rock opera called *Tommy*. The movie featured Elton John and had music by The Who. Brad was 12 and had just discovered rock-and-roll. He already owned an album by The Who and was on his way to becoming an Elton John fan. He loved the movie's score and star so much that he saw the film twice.

BRAD PITT

Paul Newman and Robert Redford in Butch Cassidy and the Sundance Kid

By the time he was a teenager, Brad was hooked on cinema. He saw all the hit films of the late 1970s as well as classics from the past. Two of his favorites were *Saturday Night Fever*, which starred John Travolta as a disco dancer, and *Ordinary People*, about a troubled

A Missouri Childhood

A scene from Planet of the Apes

family. But it was a thought-provoking thriller called *Planet of the Apes* that left the deepest impression.

Planet of the Apes was unlike any film Brad had ever seen. Set in the distant future, it tells the story of an astronaut whose spaceship crashes onto an unknown planet. The planet is inhabited by both humanlike creatures and apes. But in a surprising twist, it is the apes who are in charge and the humans who are kept in cages.

BRAD PITT

It isn't until the end of the film that the identity of the planet is revealed. In what Brad describes as one of the greatest movie moments of all time, the camera focuses on a familiar-looking structure buried in sand. Slowly both the astronaut and the audience come to realize that the structure is America's own Statue of Liberty and that the Planet of the Apes is actually planet Earth.

Brad was excited by the ideas the movie explored about society and freedom. Even more he was dazzled by the imagination of the filmmakers. It was his first understanding of the power of film. It was perhaps this movie more than any other that would later influence his decision to act.

But despite his deep interest in cinema, when it came time for college, Brad still had no thought of studying acting. By then he had become convinced that his true calling was art.

Brad's senior-year photo from the 1982 Kickapoo High School yearbook

CHAPTER

3

A Daring Decision

In 1982 Brad entered the University of Missouri at Columbia. His plan was to earn a degree in journalism, graduate, and then get a job writing for an advertising agency. He hoped eventually to work his way up in the company to the position of art director. He had always liked to draw, and he had always been good at it. But until the months before his graduation from high school, drawing had been just another one of the many things he enjoyed.

Around the age of 17, Brad discovered that his feeling for art had deepened. Alert to the artistic possibilities around him, he began to carry a notebook and pencil in his pocket for quick sketches of things that caught his eye. He also spent time in museums and galleries, studying the work of the great painters. He thought that a career in art advertising would be a wonderful means of self-expression. The University of Missouri seemed to be the right place to begin his preparation.

The School of Journalism at the University of Missouri

The campus of the University of Missouri at Columbia

BRAD PITT

The University of Missouri library

had an outstanding reputation. In addition to being the oldest journalism school in the country, it had a comprehensive program that required long hours of serious study to complete. Brad worked hard and did well.

Friends who watched him during the years that he attended the school were impressed by his single-mindedness and by his dedication to his chosen course. There was no doubt in anyone's mind that Brad would

A Daring Decision

complete his degree, settle down to a promising job in his field, and then later marry and raise a family, probably in Missouri. Brad seemed to believe it, too. Then one day, just two credits short of his degree, to everyone's astonishment he quit.

In the December 1, 1994, issue of *Rolling Stone*, Brad explained his action by saying, "I was coming to the end of college and the end of my degree and the beginning of my chosen occupation. I knew I didn't want to do it." He went on to tell *People* magazine in the January 30, 1995, issue, "I decided everyone was applying for a job or getting married, and I didn't want to do either."

Although the decision to abandon his plans had been made in an instant, it had taken weeks for Brad to realize that he had chosen the wrong course. "You keep finding things in little increments," he explained in the February 1995 issue of *Vanity Fair* magazine. "Each one of those little increments led me to saying, 'You know what? I don't want to do this.'"

But rather than feeling that his time in college had been wasted, Brad credits the experience with helping to set him straight. "I had a great time in college," he said in the same *Vanity Fair* article. "I learned more about being on my own than anything from a book. It's just as important to find out what you don't want to do as what you do want to do."

However, at that point, what Brad wanted to do was unclear. The only thing that was certain was that he was ready to break free—to do something adventurous and fun. That meant leaving Missouri to see new places and try new things. "You don't really get it into your head that you can leave," Brad said in *Rolling Stone*'s May 14, 1992, issue. "Not too many people leave. Till it was about time to graduate and it just dawned on me—'I can leave.' It would be so simple, so easy."

But where would he go? He let his instincts direct him. "You load up the car," he explained, and "you point it west"—west to Hollywood, California, the land of movie magic.

CHAPTER

4

Making It in Hollywood

It was spring of 1986 when Brad set off for Hollywood. It was a long journey, but Brad loved every minute of the ride. As he drove across the vast stretches of open land that marked the states of Oklahoma, Texas, New Mexico, and Arizona, he felt his expectations growing. "I remember being so excited as I passed each state line," he said in the December 1, 1994, issue of *Rolling Stone*.

However, once he arrived in California, he felt a little let down. "I drove in through Burbank," he recalled in the same article, "and the smog was so thick that it seemed like fog. I pulled in and went to McDonald's, and that was it. I just thought, 'Shouldn't there be a little more?'" What Brad had realized was that just being in the place of his dreams wasn't enough. It would take time and effort to make a movie career happen.

With just $325 in his pocket, Brad rented a tiny apartment and set out to find work. He was willing to try anything to support himself while attempting to break into films. During the weeks that followed, he had

BRAD PITT

This famous sign sits high atop the Hollywood hills.

a series of brief and unpleasant jobs that at least helped him meet his expenses.

First he delivered refrigerators to college students. The job required loading the refrigerators onto trucks, unloading them at their destinations, then hauling them down dormitory corridors. The work was exhausting, and Brad was glad when the job was completed.

He was next employed as a telemarketer. His task was to sell tickets to a police fund-raiser over the phone. The job proved to be a lot harder than it sounded. Most of the people Brad called either hung up on him or scolded him for disturbing them. It was no fun at all, so after a short time he quit.

Making It in Hollywood

After that he put on a chicken costume and went to work for El Pollo Loco, a fast-food restaurant specializing in chicken. His assignment was to stand outside the restaurant in his chicken suit, flap his wings, and make clucking sounds as a way to lure in customers. The suit was hot and the work was humiliating. It wasn't long before he "flew the coop."

All the while that he was going from one job to another, Brad was also attending acting auditions in his spare time. He soon managed to get a spot as an extra in a movie called *Less Than Zero*. He would be on-screen for just a second as part of a crowd in a room. But it was a start and Brad was happy.

"At the time, it was all exciting," he said in the May 14, 1992, issue of *Rolling Stone*. It was also a very different life from what he would have had if he'd stayed in Missouri. Back home he was close to lakes and hills, and he missed that. But Hollywood was an adventure. What Brad didn't know was that the best part of that adventure was yet to come.

It began while he was working as a chauffeur for a limousine company. One of his passengers had a friend who was an actor. As Brad drove the woman to her destination, he began to talk with her about the best way to

BRAD PITT

forge a movie career. The woman suggested that Brad get an acting coach. She recommended her friend's coach, Roy London, who was well-known in Hollywood circles. Roy had worked with some of Hollywood's biggest stars. Brad contacted Roy and became a pupil in his class.

Brad learned a lot from Roy about the difference between real life and life on-screen. He discovered that things people do automatically in their everyday lives must be done differently on film. There were lessons in how to breathe, how to stand and move, and how to deliver lines in front of a camera. Brad worked hard and absorbed information fast. With Roy's help he began to uncover his natural talent and to develop it to the fullest. His efforts paid off. When his first acting opportunity came, he was ready.

The opportunity was a chance to perform a scene in front of a Hollywood agent. Agents are important, powerful people in the movie business. With ties to producers, directors, scriptwriters, casting offices, and the major motion-picture studios, they can serve as a vital link between the movie industry and the individual actor. Once an agent agrees to represent an actor, that actor has a very good chance of getting work.

Making It in Hollywood

    Brad made the most of the opportunity, even though it had actually been arranged for someone else. A woman in his acting class needed a partner for an audition she had arranged for herself with an acting agency. She invited Brad to go along merely as a supporting player. Brad was simply supposed to say his lines and disappear. But he handled himself so well that the agency signed him instead of the woman. A month later he was offered his first role on a popular television series called *Dallas*. Although it wasn't a movie role, it was a giant step up the Hollywood ladder.

    In 1987, Brad appeared in five *Dallas* episodes—enough to get noticed. He began to be recognized in public and to get his first fan letters, mostly from females. Teen magazines also started to feature him in articles. Best of all, he was offered more roles. Although the work that came to him as a result of his *Dallas* success continued to be for television, Brad could hardly complain. No longer did he have to depend on refrigerator deliveries, cranky telephone customers, chicken suits, or limousines for his living. He was an acknowledged working actor. In seven short months he had achieved what most other aspiring actors never attain.

Brad, about the time of his appearance on TV's Dallas

CHAPTER

5

Television and Movies

One of the first things Brad did after winning the role on *Dallas* was phone home with the news. He was nervous about the call. Although he had remained in close touch with his parents since his arrival in Hollywood, he had been deliberately vague about what he was actually doing there. Fearing that his mother and father would worry if they knew he was pursuing an acting career, he had allowed them to think that he was studying art at a nearby college. But with *Dallas* the time had come to tell them the truth.

To Brad's astonishment his parents seemed to have known the truth all along. Brad told *Rolling Stone* in the December 1, 1994, issue that his father responded to the news by saying, "Yeah, I thought so." Brad's mother had told the same magazine in the May 14, 1992, issue that no one in the family was the least bit surprised by Brad's change of career plans. "He's just someone who's always liked to try new things," she explained.

But word of Brad's show-business success did startle

BRAD PITT

Brad with his parents

Television and Movies

his university friends. An old college pal, interviewed for *Rolling Stone*'s December 1, 1994, issue, said, "People at Missouri [University] were really surprised when they found out what Brad had been doing. But he's always been so charming that it made some sense." And that charm of which Brad's friends spoke would become more and more evident to more and more people in weeks to come.

After *Dallas*, Brad did a one-week stint on *Another World*, a daytime drama taped in New York. It was his first trip to the city, and he was captivated by the sights. He was especially thrilled at the chance to visit New York's world-famous museums and galleries. Still intensely interested in art, he had continued to draw and sketch whenever he could.

After that it was back to California, where he auditioned for television sitcoms. He got guest-starring roles on *Growing Pains* and *Head of the Class*, two very popular shows of the late 1980s. He also played a dramatic part on *21 Jump Street*, another highly watched program. In whatever Brad did, his talent and charm were apparent. The *21 Jump Street* producer told *People* magazine in its January 30, 1995, issue that even in his earliest days, Brad was impossible to ignore. "Brad walking into a room," he said, "was more exciting than most actors doing a scene." The producer of *thirtysomething*, another popular television drama in which Brad appeared, echoed that same feeling in the same magazine article. "He caused such a stir on the set," the *thirtysomething* producer said of Brad. "He was so good-looking and so charismatic and such a sweet guy, everybody knew he was going places."

But after a while, Brad began to wonder exactly where he was headed. He seemed to be on his way to a career in television, which was not his original plan. Although his agent advised him to stay on the television course, believing that he had a better chance there than in films, Brad continued to follow his heart. When he was offered the starring role in a teen comedy-horror movie, he took it.

The film was called *Cutting Class*. Brad now admits that it was just awful. The public and critics seemed to agree. *Cutting Class* failed at the box office and disappeared from movie theaters within a few weeks of its release.

Determined to try again, Brad immediately signed on for another movie, this one called *Happy Together*. Once again it was a comedy, and once again it was a flop. With two failures in a row, Brad had every reason to feel discouraged. Instead he took it all in stride, simply putting

Television and Movies

his movie dreams on hold and returning to television. He saw television as a way to keep working as he waited for better movie offers to come along.

In 1990 he did a small part in a TV film called *The Image*. He followed that with a major role in another television movie entitled *Too Young to Die?* Playing a small-time hood, he was so believably evil that his own family hardly knew him. It was the first time that Brad's parents had seen him in such a sustained and unpleasant role. Brad's work in *Too Young to Die?* surely convinced Bill and Jane Pitt that their son had talent and that his career choice had been sound.

After that Brad went to work for the Fox Television Network. He was one of four young actors hired to costar on *Glory Days*, a series about a group of friends and their lives after high school. The success of Fox's *Beverly Hills 90210* had convinced the network that programs about young and good-looking people went over well with the public. Everyone connected with *Glory Days* expected it to be a big hit. Six episodes were taped and then aired in July of 1990. But for reasons that are not clear, the show never caught on. No further episodes were shot, and by September the show had been canceled.

Undaunted by the show's failure, Brad forged on.

BRAD PITT

Brad and costar Juliette Lewis in Too Young to Die?

He even came to view the program's lack of success as a blessing. Had *Glory Days* become a hit, he would not have been free to accept the next movie role he was offered. The movie was called *Across the Tracks*, and it gave Brad his first major cinematic role.

Across the Tracks tells the story of two brothers

The cast of Glory Days

BRAD PITT

Brad and actor Rick Schroder in a scene from Across the Tracks

competing for the track championship of their county. Brad played quiet, serious Joe, and former child-star Rick Schroder played Joe's troubled brother, Billy. Much of the film centered around the brothers' often tense, often loving relationship, both on and off the track. As the introverted Joe, Brad had to convey his character's feelings through facial expressions and body movements.

Television and Movies

It was a true test of his dramatic skills, which did not go unnoticed by the press. Although the film was not a commercial success, Brad's sensitive performance earned him favorable reviews. A critic for the May 23, 1990, edition of *Variety*, an important entertainment periodical, summed up the feelings of many when he praised Brad for being "excellent in a complex role."

Part of Brad's preparation for the film involved physical training. In order to be convincing as a runner, he had to spend weeks prior to shooting doing daily laps around the track. By the time the cameras were ready to roll, he was able to run like a true athlete. But the work was exhausting, particularly because the track scenes were shot outdoors under California's blazing summer sun.

Brad's next role was smaller, less complex, and much less physically taxing. But it was the one that would make him a star.

CHAPTER 6

J.D. and Beyond

In 1991 Brad auditioned for a part in a big-budget movie called *Thelma and Louise*. The movie would feature Geena Davis and Susan Sarandon as two friends out for adventure. The character that interested Brad was a southern hitchhiker named J.D., whom Thelma and Louise pick up along the way. The part of J.D. was actually minor, amounting only to about 15 minutes on-screen. But Brad believed it was a role he had been born to play.

"I figured it would be a role like J.D.—something I'm good at, a southern guy—that would make the break," he told *Rolling Stone* in its May 14, 1992, issue. He couldn't have been more right.

Four hundred actors tried out for the part. Brad not only got it, but his work left a lasting impression on the film's casting director, Lou DiGiaimo. Based on Brad's audition alone, Lou predicted that Brad was headed for superstardom.

And yet, in a way, *Thelma and Louise* was a risk.

Brad as the hitchhiking J.D. in Thelma and Louise

BRAD PITT

For decades, Hollywood producers had been gearing their films toward men, who made up the bulk of movie audiences. Male action, adventure, and "buddy" films featuring stars like Arnold Schwarzenegger and Sylvester Stallone had all but dominated the nation's movie screens. *Thelma and Louise* would be a departure from this type of Hollywood film. Not only would it star women, but it would show them in strong and daring roles. No one who worked on the film—not the producers, not the director, not Brad himself—knew if such a film would have a chance at the box office.

To everyone's surprise, *Thelma and Louise* not only survived but went on to become a hit. Women in particular flocked to the nation's movie theaters, eager to see the film. After years of being ignored by the movie industry, women across the United States felt a new sense of power and importance. Most loved seeing Geena Davis and Susan Sarandon playing characters who took hold of their lives with much the same strength and determination as men. And perhaps even more, they loved watching Brad.

Despite Brad's small role, his impact on female moviegoers was phenomenal. Younger and older women alike were captivated by his charm and good

J.D and Beyond

Brad with Thelma and Louise *star Geena Davis*

looks. A combination of positive word-of-mouth and favorable reviews brought him the kind of notice that does wonders for a film career. *Thelma and Louise* was Brad's ticket to the top.

The movie went on to be nominated for several Academy Awards. It also won a place on *Entertainment Weekly*'s list of the 100 most popular films of all time.

BRAD PITT

By the time it was released on video, it had generated so much interest and talk that even men were eager to see it. With each new round of *Thelma and Louise*'s success, Brad's movie-star status seemed secured.

After *Thelma and Louise*, Brad had no difficulty getting parts. Day after day, scripts and movie offers flooded his mailbox. However, most of the roles he was offered were simply variations of the J.D. character. Brad could have chosen to play it safe and make a career of these J.D. variations. Instead, he looked for new and different characters in projects that challenged him. Four such projects came his way in 1992.

The first of these was *Johnny Suede*. Putting his star status on the line, Brad jumped at the chance to play in this small offbeat movie. The film, which Brad made purely to satisfy himself, was truly a labor of love. Far too quirky for mainstream movie theaters, *Johnny Suede* would run in art houses—small theaters that feature unusual films—and at film festivals. Brad knew that the film would not draw crowds, would not earn him huge sums of money, and would do little to further his movie career. But *Johnny Suede* was the story of a musician. And playing the title role would give Brad a chance to explore the strange and wild world of rock-and-roll.

J.D and Beyond

Brad as rock-and-roller Johnny Suede

Over the years, Brad's childhood love of rock-and-roll had developed into a passion. By the time he arrived in Hollywood, he had acquired a large collection of rock-and-roll recordings. He had also learned to play the harmonica and the guitar. In addition, even after he began acting full time, he made time for jam sessions with friends. There were even moments when he wondered what it would be like to be a professional musician. *Johnny Suede* was a way for him to experience the musician's life without actually living it. The role left him with a new understanding of the problems involved in the music business. Although it in no way diminished his feeling for rock-and-roll, the work made him glad he had decided to become an actor.

Following *Johnny Suede*, Brad appeared in yet another offbeat movie called *Cool World*. The film was a mixture of live action and animation, with Brad playing the role of a detective whose job it was to keep the human and cartoon worlds apart. Critics found the film too focused on cartoon action and color at the expense of storytelling and plot. As a result, the movie was not a commercial success.

But for Brad, *Cool World* was less a failure than an opportunity to work in a whole new way. Because most of his scenes were with cartoon characters that would be drawn in later, he had to act alone. Playing with invisible costars in an empty room was an unusual challenge. The experience stretched his dramatic talents as never before.

After *Cool World* Brad took on his most important role to date. It was the lead part in a major commercial

J.D and Beyond

Brad with one of his "costars" in the animated Cool World

movie called *A River Runs Through It*. There was much about the project that appealed to Brad. The film was set in Montana and was shot mostly out-of-doors. The character he portrayed was interesting and complex. And the film's director was Robert Redford, whom Brad had admired since childhood. Not only had Robert Redford starred in *Butch Cassidy and the Sundance Kid*, but he had also directed *Ordinary People*, another of Brad's early film favorites.

BRAD PITT

A River Runs Through It is the story of a family whose members share a love of fly-fishing. Brad's character, Paul Maclean, is the younger and more daring of two brothers. On the outside, Paul seems well adjusted and full of fun. But inside, he is sad and deeply troubled about his life and his relationship with his father. The role required Brad to show Paul's charming exterior while also suggesting the dark, disturbing depths that lay beneath.

In addition to its acting challenges, the role also required fly-fishing expertise. In preparation, Brad spent weeks prior to filming perfecting his fishing skills. Hour after hour, day after day, he practiced casting his rod. More than once he came close to disaster. "I'd hook myself in the back of my head all the time," he told *Rolling Stone* in May of 1992. "One time, they had to dig the barb out with pliers." But his perseverance paid off. The grace and beauty of Brad's fly-fishing scenes are among the film's highlights.

A River Runs Through It did well at the box office, even though critics were divided on its merit. The one thing on which both reviewers and moviegoers agreed was Brad's startling resemblance to the film's director. In the October 18, 1992, edition of *The New York Times*, writer Caryn James put into words what many had

For his role in A River Runs Through It, *Brad had to perfect his fishing skills.*

BRAD PITT

thought. "Mr. Pitt looks astonishingly like the young Robert Redford," she said, "with the same mischievous grin and crinkly smile." The comparison must have pleased Brad. It would have been understandable had he decided to play up his Robert Redford likeness. Instead, he deliberately chose to play against it.

Against the advice of his agents, Brad followed the part of Paul Maclean with the role of a villain named Early Grayce in a movie called *Kalifornia*. Not only was the appearance and manner of the Early Grayce character a complete contrast to Paul's (and to Robert Redford's), but the low-budget film was a step down the Hollywood ladder. It was a rare move indeed for an actor at the pinnacle of his success.

Brad put his heart and soul into the villainous role, gaining 20 pounds, letting his hair grow long, sprouting a goatee, and acquiring a stoop-shouldered walk. His appearance alone was so scraggly and menacing that it totally erased any thought of Robert Redford or Paul Maclean. It has been said that both Brad and the film may have gone too far in their depiction of evil. *Kalifornia* did not fare well at the box office. However, Brad was not upset. The Early Grayce role had helped him accomplish his goal, even if it hadn't pleased audiences.

J.D and Beyond

The Favor *did not fare well at the box office*

Two more unsuccessful films followed—*True Romance*, in 1993, and *The Favor*, a year later. Then Brad appeared in what would become two of 1994's biggest hits—*Legends of the Fall* and *Interview With the Vampire*. Together these movies would propel him back to the height of stardom.

CHAPTER 7

The Actor and the Man

"I've always thought there would be someone better for most of the roles I've taken," Brad told *Vanity Fair* in February of 1995, when speaking about his part in *Legends of the Fall*. "But I knew I was the best one to play Tristan. I knew it the minute I read it. I knew the corners, the bends in the road, knew exactly where it went." In fact, Brad so related to the role that he invested a portion of his $3 million salary in the film's production.

Tristan is *Legends of the Fall*'s lead character. One of three brothers in a close-knit Montana family, he is handsome, charming, and wild—more likely to be ruled by his heart than by his head. Through a series of tragic events, he comes to understand himself and his place in the universe. The film is a journey of self-discovery, which Brad found to be both accurate and true. In the same *Vanity Fair* article, Brad described the film as being about "sinking below, rising above, going off, giving up, taking charge, taking control"—things about which he knew quite a bit. His close identification with the character he

Brad as Tristan in Legends of the Fall

BRAD PITT

The cast of Legends of the Fall. *Brad is seated between actors Aiden Quinn and Henry Thomas. Julia Ormond is to the right.*

portrayed made his performance that much more stirring.

Released in December of 1994, *Legends of the Fall* thrilled moviegoers, largely because of Brad's portrayal. He was called "effortlessly charismatic" by *Variety* in its December 19, 1994, issue. The *Chicago Tribune*, in its January 13, 1995, edition, compared him with the legendary James Dean, a movie megastar of the 1950s. The film was a success, earning more than $60 million in its first two months. But even more rewarding for Brad, his

The Actor and the Man

performance won him a Golden Globe nomination.

Immediately after completing *Legends of the Fall*, Brad began filming *Interview With the Vampire*. The movie was based on a popular novel that Brad had read and enjoyed. Had he known how unpleasant the work would be, he might never have accepted the part.

Filming Interview with the Vampire *was a difficult experience for Brad.*

Brad played an eighteenth-century plantation owner whose grief over the deaths of his wife and daughter leads him to become a vampire. It was a grim role, made all the more difficult by the filming schedule. The movie took five-and-a-half months to shoot. Forty of the shooting sessions were at night, to create a dark, eerie feeling. The intense pace and continual lack of light gave Brad little relief from both the film's and his character's troubled mood. To his credit he stayed with the project to the end. But it was an unhappy experience and his first movie that was not fun to do.

"It affected me," he told *Vanity Fair* in February of 1995 when discussing his vampire role. "It messed with my day." He went on to explain, "Somewhere in the third or fourth week [of filming a movie], you respond to things a little differently, like your character would respond. I don't like it. I can't wait to get my own clothes back on, listen to some good music, eat what I want to eat. Movies are very complicated. You don't realize what it takes to get a good movie. Sitting home in Missouri, I sure didn't."

Despite the difficulties, Brad was pleased with the finished film. And so were the fans. *Interview With the Vampire* earned $105 million in the first three months of its release. Reviewer Caryn James of *The New York Times* was one of many who credited Brad for the film's success. On November 13, 1994, she wrote that the power of the movie depended on Brad's "rich and deeply affecting performance."

With two highly successful motion pictures in the same year, Brad was more popular and in demand than

The Actor and the Man

ever. His salary climbed to $6 million per project. Film offers came in faster than he could handle them, and fans swamped him at every turn.

In the years since the release of *Legends of the Fall* and *Interview With the Vampire*, Brad has gone on to star in a series of box-office hits. Together they have solidified his superstar status. Among his recent and highly successful films are *Seven*, in which he played a big-city cop; *12 Monkeys*, for which he won a Golden Globe award; and *Sleepers*, which teamed him with Robert De Niro and Dustin Hoffman, two of Hollywood's most respected actors.

Brad arriving at the New York premiere of Seven

He also starred in a 1997 thriller called *The Devil's Own*, in which he played an Irish rebel. Like *Interview With the Vampire*, *The Devil's Own* proved to be a

55

BRAD PITT

difficult project. Much of the problem centered around the screenplay, which Brad had first read in 1991 and loved. As originally written, Brad's character was tough, gritty, and mean, the kind of real-life antihero that appealed to him, but that mainstream Hollywood movies rarely feature. Brad had no idea when he signed on for the role that both the script and his character would be drastically changed.

In an effort to make the film acceptable to mainstream movie audiences, studio executives hired a group of writers to soften the screenplay. By the time shooting began, only twenty pages of the original script remained. Even worse, Brad's character had been transformed from a disagreeable "bad guy" into a more traditional Hollywood hero. Only the threat of a $63 million lawsuit kept Brad from walking off the set.

In an uncharacteristic display of anger, the usually mild-mannered Brad lashed out at the studio in a much-quoted interview with *Newsweek* magazine. In the magazine's February 3, 1997, issue, he called *The Devil's Own* "the most irresponsible bit of filmmaking" that he had ever seen. Later, when his temper had cooled, he retracted his statement.

But despite Brad's initially negative words, the movie

The Actor and the Man

got good reviews and did well at the box-office. *Entertainment Weekly* noted in its April 11, 1997, issue that only a superstar of Brad's magnitude could speak against his own film and not kill box-office sales.

Another film released in 1997 was *Seven Years in Tibet*, in which Brad played real-life mountain climber Heinrich Harrer. Shot in a remote town in Argentina, the movie brought Brad a different kind of challenge.

Brad in The Devil's Own

Argentine movie fans, thrilled at having a Hollywood superstar in their midst, went wild with excitement. Mobs of young girls congregated outside the local restaurant where Brad ate, banging on the windows and chanting his name. In order to protect the premises, the restaurant's

BRAD PITT

owner had to install partitions, dark windows, and dimmer lights inside. A similar frenzy broke out in front of the house where Brad stayed. It took the addition of a $30,000 wall around the property to give him the quiet and privacy he desired. The company producing the film assumed the cost, yet another indication of Brad's superstar status.

It is not surprising that the more famous Brad Pitt becomes, the more willing the world's movie producers are to spend money on him. The film *Meet Joe Black* will earn him $17.5 million, his highest salary to date. Loosely based on a 1934 Hollywood classic, *Death Takes a Holiday*, the movie should also suit Brad's offbeat taste. For the first time in his career, he plays the role of the grim reaper.

As his reputation has grown, Brad has become as visible on television and in print as he is on film. Nightly entertainment shows run regular stories about him. Magazine and newspaper reporters hound him for interviews. And photographers pop up out of nowhere to snap his picture at public and private functions.

With media and fans watching his every move, Brad has had a particularly difficult time keeping his romantic involvements secret. His recent off-screen relationship

The Actor and the Man

with actress Gwyneth Paltrow was the subject of Hollywood gossip for weeks. The two met in 1995 on the set of *Seven*. (Gwyneth played Brad's wife in the film.) As soon as they began to date, they were bombarded with questions about their intentions. Barely able to withstand the pressure, they soon revealed all. In December 1996, Gwyneth joined Brad in Argentina, where they announced their engagement. Not long after, they also told of their plans to star together in a movie. The film, entitled *Duets*, would be directed by Hollywood producer Bruce Paltrow, Gwyneth's father.

But the couple's openness merely served to increase the public's hunger for information. Reporters and fans continued to dog their every step, allowing them little privacy or space. The intense scrutiny seems to have taken its toll. By the summer of 1997, Brad and Gwyneth had called off the engagement and also the movie.

Like most celebrities, Brad has discovered that fame has a price. But he has also found his own unique way of dealing with it. These days, when he isn't working on a film, he is most likely to be at home, far removed from the public spotlight.

More than fancy hotels or exotic vacation spots, home has long been Brad's favorite place to relax and unwind.

BRAD PITT

In October 1994, Brad told *Premiere* magazine that his home was "very, very important," especially as his fame grew and became harder and harder to manage. Today, with his popularity at an all-time high, home has become more important to him than ever. It is, in fact, so vital to his well-being that he has devoted himself to making it as comfortable as possible, personally undertaking its maintenance and decoration. Fans may find it hard to believe that the same actor who can light up a movie screen with his mere presence enjoys spending his time off washing dishes and polishing furniture.

Brad also enjoys such other at-home activities as reading, sketching, playing his guitar, listening to CDs, and watching old movies on TV. His new dream is to build a house in Missouri to use as a place for family reunions. To that end, he has put much of his film earnings into the purchase of land in the Ozarks.

For all his success, wealth, and fame, Brad remains true to his Missouri roots. Friends, family members, and people with whom he has worked all have high praise for his character and kindness.

In the January 30, 1995, issue of *People* magazine, Brad's brother, Doug, described Brad as "a regular Joe." In the same magazine, Brad's *Legends of the Fall* costar

The Actor and the Man

Julia Ormond marveled that despite Brad's achievements, he is very modest and sweet. And Terry Gilliam, who directed Brad in *12 Monkeys*, offered an equally glowing assessment of the actor and the man. Interviewed for *People*'s December 25, 1995, year-end issue, in which Brad was named one of the year's 25 most intriguing people, Gilliam described Brad as "a decent, good guy who's serious about his work."

How does Brad view himself? His own words from *Rolling Stone*'s December 1, 1994, issue express it best.

About his acting, Brad says, "I'm a good actor, I'm consistent, but I'll never be a great actor. Every now and then I'll be great. Every now and then I'll be lousy."

And on the way he lives his life, Brad offers this candid assessment. "I have to use a cheesy word," he cautions, "but I'd say I try to guide my life by honesty. And that's a hard thing. I haven't mastered it by any means."

Maybe he hasn't. But being Brad, he is well on his way.

INDEX

Academy Awards, 41
Across the Tracks, 34–37
animation, 44, 45
Another World, 31
Butch Cassidy and the Sundance Kid, 13, 14, 45
Cool World, 44, 45
Cutting Class, 32
Dallas, 27, 29
Davis, Geena, 38, 40, *41*
Devil's Own, The, 55–57
DiGiaimo, Lou, 38
Duets, 59
fans, 57–59
Favor, The, 49
fly-fishing, 46
Fox Television Network, 33
Gilliam, Terry, 61
Glory Days, 33–35
Golden Globe, 53, 55
Growing Pains, 31
Happy Together, 32
Harrer, Heinrich, 57
Head of the Class, 31
Hollywood, 7, 22, 23, *24*, 25
Image, The, 33
Interview With the Vampire, 49, 53–54
Johnny Suede, 42–44
Kalifornia, 48
Legends of the Fall, 49, 50–53, 60
Less than Zero, 25
London, Roy, 26
Meet Joe Black, 58
Ormond, Julia, 60–61
Paltrow, Bruce, 59
Paltrow, Gwyneth, 59
Pitt, Bill, 9, 10, 11, 12–13, 29, *30*, 33
Pitt, Brad: acting lessons, 26; at home, 59–60; auditions, 25, 26–27; childhood, 9–16; college, 18–21; jobs, 24–26; movie roles, 7, 25, 33, 36–37, 38–49, 50–58; musical activities, 10, 11, 13, 42–44; salary, 50, 55, 58; TV roles, 7, 27, 29, 31, 33
Pitt, Doug, 9, 60

Pitt, Jane, 9, 10, 13, 29, *30*, 33
Pitt, Julie, 9
Planet of the Apes, 15–16
Redford, Robert, 13, 14, 45, 48
River Runs Through It, A, 45–48
Sarandon, Susan, 38, 40
Seven, 55, 59
Seven Years in Tibet, 57
Sleepers, 55
Thelma and Louise, 38–42
thirtysomething, 32
Tommy, 13
Too Young to Die?, 33
True Romance, 49
12 Monkeys, 55, 61
21 Jump Street, 31
University of Missouri, 18–20, 31

ABOUT THE AUTHOR

Paula Guzzetti spent the first part of her professional life teaching grades kindergarten through eight. Now a full-time writer, she has a special interest in history, literature, and the arts. In addition to *Brad Pitt*, Paula's books for children include *Jim Carrey*, also in the Taking Part series; *A Family Called Brontë*; and *The White House*. Paula has also completed biographies of Hawaiian Queen Liliuokalani, Texas hero Sam Houston, and ballerina Maria Tallchief.